Wild Weather

Julie Haydon

Contents

Rigby

The Weather

When we think of the weather, we think of sunshine or rain.

But sometimes the weather is wild!

It can wreck buildings.
It can hurt people
and animals.

Wild weather
can even change
the way the land looks.

Floods

Animals and plants need water to live, but sometimes there is too much water.

5

When there is too much water,
rivers can overflow.
The water **floods** the land.

Rivers flood because of heavy rain
and melting snow.

The sea can flood, too.
It can flood the land
along the **coast**.

The sea floods when storms make strong winds
and big waves.

Drought

When it does not rain
for a long time,
there is not enough water
for animals and plants.
The land dries out.
This is a **drought**.

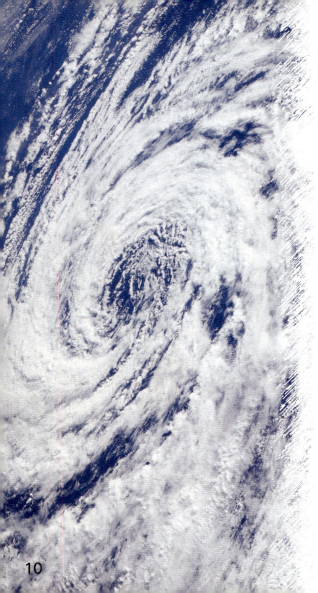

Cyclones

Cyclones are wild storms. Many cyclones begin over warm oceans.

When cyclones reach land, they bring strong winds, rain, **hail,** and lightning.

Cyclones make huge waves
in the ocean.
These waves can crash
onto the land and flood it.

Cyclones are so strong,
they can knock over buildings.

Studying the Weather

People can study the weather.
People who study
the weather
are called **meteorologists**.
They use photographs,
special tools, and computers
to help them.

Meteorologists can warn us
when wild weather
is on the way.

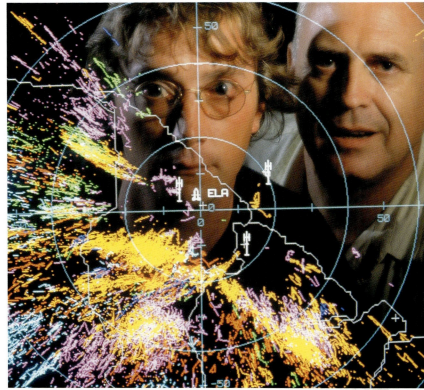

Glossary

coast land next to the sea

cyclones wild storms with strong winds, heavy rain, hail, and lightning

drought when it does not rain for a long time

floods overflows onto land

hail small balls of ice that fall from clouds

meteorologists people who study the weather

Index